LETTERS FROM
BEYOND THE SAMBATYON

≈

THE MYTH OF THE TEN LOST TRIBES

Edited by Simcha Shtull-Trauring

m a x i m a
N E W   M E D I A

Published by MAXIMA New Media Ltd.
2472 Broadway / Suite 195
New York, NY 10025
Tel: (212) 439-4177
Fax: (212) 439-4178
Orders: (800) 231-3070
e-mail: info@maxnm.com
website: http://www.maxnm.com/

Development Office:
P.O.B. 1195
Kokhav Yair 44864
ISRAEL

Art director and designer: Orit Kariv-Manor

Historical advisor: Dr. Geoffrey Wigoder, Editor-in-Chief of Encyclopaedia Judaica;
Historical advisor, Beth Hatefutsoth (The Nahum Goldmann Museum of the
Jewish Diaspora, Tel Aviv)

Grateful acknowledgment is made and special thanks are due to the following
authors, translators (living and dead), and publishers for use of their publications
for the reproduction of letters:
1. E.N. Adler, *Jewish Travellers,* George Routledge & Sons, London, 1931
2. H. Adler, *Miscellany of Hebrew Literature,* London, 1872
3. Joseph Kastein, *The Messiah of Ismir, Sabatai Zevi,*
    translated by Huntley Patterson, London, 1931
4. Franz Kobler, *Letters of Jews through the Ages,* Jewish Publication Society, 1978
5. Cecil Roth, *The Life of Menasseh ben Israel,* Jewish Publications Society, 1934
6. *The Jewish Caravan* by Leo Schwarz. Copyright © 1965 by Leo Schwarz.
    Reprinted by permission of Henry Holt & Company, Inc.

Book illustrations based on 16th-19th century maps.
Illustration, pg. 46: The legendary Christian king Prester John
(From: *The Prester John of the Indies* by F. Alvares. Lisbon, 1540).

Library of Congress Catalog Card Number: 96-94695
Publisher's Cataloging in Publication
   (Prepared by Quality Books Inc.)

Letters from beyond the Sambatyon: the myth of the ten lost tribes /
   ed., Simcha Shtull-Trauring
   p. cm.
   ISBN: 1-888297-03-4

   1. Lost tribes of Israel.   I. Shtull-Trauring, Simcha

DS131.L48 1997   909'.04'924
                                              QBI96-40240

CONTENTS

PAGE

The Myth of the Ten Lost Tribes 5

Letters from Beyond the Sambatyon 7

The Letters

1. The Roman Emperor and the Sluggish Sabbath-Breaker
   (Flavius Josephus, 1st century) 13

2. Wicked Cannibals, 32 Gold Pieces
   (Eldad the Danite, 883 CE) 17

3. Curiosity and the Spanish Diplomat
   (Hisdai ibn Shaprut, c960) 25

4. Learned Men and Savage Warriors
   (Benjamin of Tudela, 12th cent.) 31

5. In Search of Paradise
   (Obadiah Jare of Bertinoro, 1488-1489) 37

6. A Visit to the Pope (David Reubeni, c1525) 43

7. Where the Waters Run Sacred
   (Gershon Yiddls of Prague, 1624) 51

8. The Native Americans and the Second Coming
   (Menasseh ben Israel, 1649) 57

9. Behold, the Messiah! (Nathan of Gaza, 1665) 61

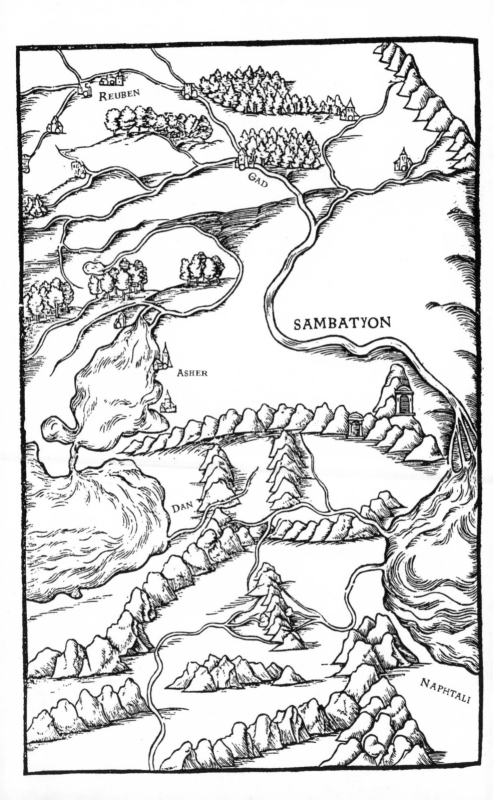

The Myth of the Ten Lost Tribes

Sarah Harel-Hoshen

The Ten Lost Tribes of Israel have stirred the imagination of people from time immemorial. We know that in the 8th century BCE the Assyrian Empire destroyed the Kingdom of Israel and exiled its inhabitants. We even know from the Bible some of the places to which they were deported. That is all we know. Yet the Ten Tribes have continued to dwell in the realm between fact and fantasy ever since. For the Jewish people, their memory has been preserved in the collective consciousness as a limb severed from the body of the nation and expected to rejoin it in the "end of days."

Gershom Scholem, the noted contemporary authority on Jewish mysticism, wrote in his monumental work *Sabbatai Sevi* that "there was a persistent popular legendary tradition about the Lost Tribes. In times of eschatological propaganda... and milleniaristic expectation, reports combining half-true accounts of Jews in far-away countries with uninhibited imaginings would proliferate." In the time of the false messiah Shabbetai Zevi and his prophet Nathan of Gaza (17th cent.), for example, rumors were rife to the effect that the armies of the Ten Tribes were advancing from the desert to fight the Turks. There were other rumors that they were about to conquer Mecca. The stories were so persistent that in 1665 the Moslems of Tunis actually cancelled their pilgrimage to the holy city. Similar tales - heralding the arrival of the legions of the Tribes or describing their kingdom somewhere in the hinterlands of Asia or Africa - have surfaced regularly since the Middle Ages. They were circulated in the Middle East and Europe in letters written by Jews, in reports of Christian diplomats, or in occasional publications.

The legends, the rumors and the accounts of imaginary voyages were passed on from generation to generation. In the 16th and 17th centuries, these stories apparently played an important role in spreading messianic propaganda in the Jewish world, and in advancing the political interests of the Christian European states in their struggle against the Ottoman Empire. With the exploration of the New World, "scientific" theories began to emerge in which scholars and missionaries attempted to identify various tribes with the Ten Lost Tribes, on the basis of the similarities of their customs to Biblical traditions. Supported primarily by Anglo-American Protestant clergymen and scholars, this trend continued into the 20th century (the CD-ROM offers a look at several of these theories).

Modern anthropologists who have examined the effect of the Lost Tribes theories upon different native groups around the world, emphasize the political function which they served. Certain oppressed groups, exposed to missionary activity, identified with the Children of Israel who suffered the burden of exile and persecution, and subsequently attributed to themselves ancient Jewish origins. This would explain the Maori Jews in New Zealand, the Ashanti Jews in West Africa, and others like them. During the past two hundred years, there has been a growing trend in the Jewish world to seek out the Lost Tribes and to identify them with remote communities.

In recent years a number of individuals and organizations have continued the quest for the Lost Tribes. At the same time, several groups in South America, Asia and Africa have identified themselves as descendants of these tribes, declaring their commitment to link their fate with the Jewish people and the State of Israel.

Letters from Beyond the Sambatyon
Simcha Shtull-Trauring

Historical reality is frequently the mother of myths and, like good
offspring, myths carry on the process of creating history. We first
encounter the mighty Sabbath river, the Sambatyon (referred to
alternately as Sanbatyon and Sabatyon), in rabbinic literature. In
numerous passages we read of a river unnavigable on weekdays
when it flowed with strong currents, carrying along stones with
tremendous force; on the Sabbath, however, it rested from its fury
and lay tranquil.

In Jewish thought, the Sabbath is associated with the exodus from
Egypt, the prototype of exile and redemption. It was natural, then,
that the Rabbis connected the Sabbath River with the Assyrian
exile of the Ten Tribes of the northern kingdom of Israel in the
8th century BCE. The Jerusalem Talmud relates that "Israel was
sent into exile beyond the Sambatyon..." (Sanhedrin 10). Settle-
ment beyond a river whose name and behavior reflect the holiness
of the Sabbath day is thus symbolic of spiritual and physical exile.

The Prophets, unwilling to accept the finality of exile and
assimilation, kept alive the hope that the Ten Tribes continued to
exist, by promising the ultimate ingathering of the exiles and the
reunion of the kingdoms of Judah and Israel. The rabbinic
concepts of exile "beyond the Sambatyon" and the prophetic
promises of return together inspired a messianic quest which
persisted for centuries: the mythical river had only to be found,
and the final redemption might be expedited.

These motifs re-emerge in medieval and post-medieval Jewish folktales and writings, in which the kingdom where the Ten Tribes reside is described as the ultimate utopia, a fantasized existence which was clearly a comfort to the downtrodden Jews of the Diaspora. The Jews in this kingdom are strong, proud and fearless, often warriors, and their land overflows with precious gems, fertile livestock, exotic fruits and abundant produce.

Christian denominations with messianic aspirations were equally eager to discover such a kingdom; the existence of Israelites offered the possibility of converting them and thereby hastening the arrival of the millennium. It was inevitable that the myth of the Sambatyon became linked with a related story which appeared in the latter part of the 12th century and persisted for several centuries. According to this legend, there lived a powerful Christian priest and monarch named Prester John somewhere beyond the Moslem countries. Prester John ruled over a vast and wealthy Empire, first placed in Asia (sometimes near Armenia), but later more generally placed in Africa. More than one hundred manuscripts recounting the Prester John story have been preserved in different libraries around the world; the texts are similar to one another and all contain references to the Ten Tribes and the myth of the Sambatyon River. References to Prester John may be found in Obadiah of Bertinoro's letter (pg. 42), in the selection from David Reubeni's diary (pg. 47), and in Gershon Yiddls' travel book (pg. 54).

In this collection of writings from the 1st through the 17th century, we follow the river as it makes its way through the dreams and fantasies of travelers, scholars and theologians. As we read

Jewish historian Josephus Flavius' description of future Roman emperor Titus taking his morning walk in the 1st century, and the imaginative tales of such travelers as Eldad the Danite (9th century) and Yiddls of Prague (13th century), the Sambatyon seems to grow ever more marvelous and fantastic, taking on new forms and implications. In the 17th century, we observe the myth fashioning history in Menasseh Ben Israel's passionate plea to the ·English parliament regarding the return of the expelled Jews to England, and in the messianic proclamations of Nathan of Gaza.

In *Letters from Beyond the Sambatyon* and its accompanying CD-ROM, the echoes of an event which took place nearly 3,000 years ago resound across the world stage, carried along by the myth of a magical river.

Sarah Harel-Hoshen, curator and director of the Department of Exhibitions at the Museum of the Jewish Diaspora (Tel Aviv), has curated numerous exhibitions and edited several catalogues and publications on different aspects of Diaspora Jewry, among them "Beyond the Sambatyon: The Myth of the Ten Lost Tribes" (1991).

Simcha Shtull-Trauring worked for many years in formal and museum education, and has directed several multiple media projects. She is the co-founder of MAXIMA New Media.

The Letters

≈

The Roman Emperor and the Sluggish Sabbath-Breaker

Flavius Josephus

Jewish War 7, 1st century

Joseph ben Mattathias (better known by his Latin name, Flavius Josephus) was a leading Jewish historian of the 1st century who used the Greek language to describe the period of the destruction of the Second Temple. He owes his reputation as an historian to his two major works: The Jewish War which appeared in the years 75-59 and describes the war of the Jews against the Romans, and Jewish Antiquities which relates the history of the Jewish nation from its beginnings until just before the Great Revolt of the 1st century.

The Jewish War, from which this selection is taken, was published under the auspices of Titus, conqueror of Jerusalem and future emperor; it therefore sings the praises of the Roman Empire in general and of the Flavian dynasty (to which Titus belonged) in particular. Josephus' description of Titus' visit to the Sabbatical River is particularly interesting in that he depicts the river as one which is sluggish all week long, but stormy on the Sabbath — hence a violator of the Holy Day. This rendition contradicts the description related in the Talmud and by the 1st-century Roman naturalist Pliny — of a river which storms for six days and rests on the Sabbath.

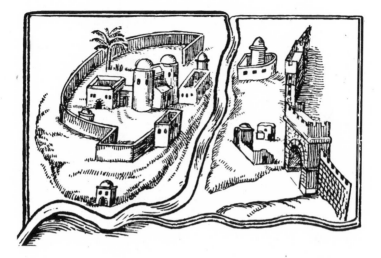

Titus Caesar, as we have already mentioned, stayed for some time at Berytus [modern Beirut]. Departing thence, he exhibited costly spectacles in all the cities of Syria through which he passed, making his Jewish captives serve to display their own destruction.

In the course of his march he saw a river, the nature of which deserves record. It runs between Arcea, a town within the realm of Agrippa [last king of the house of Herod], and Raphanea, and has an astonishing peculiarity.

For, when it flows, it is a copious stream with a current far from sluggish; then all at once its sources fail and for the space of six days it presents the spectacle of a dry bed; again, as though no change had occurred, it pours forth on the seventh day just as before. And it has always been observed to keep strictly to this order; whence they have called it the Sabbatical river, so naming it after the sacred seventh day of the Jews.

WICKED CANNIBALS,
32 GOLD PIECES

Eldad the Danite

to the Jews of Spain, 883

In the ninth century, a traveler of mysterious origins visited Jewish communities in North Africa and Spain. Calling himself Eldad the Danite, he brought news of the tribes of Dan, Naphtali, Gad and Asher allegedly residing in the land of Havilah, beyond the rivers of Ethiopia. Several European scholars question the veracity of the experiences he records in his writings (experiences which are also mentioned in other contemporary accounts), while others regard them as substantially historical.

What is certain is that he sent a letter entitled "The Lost Tribes of Israel" to the Jews of Spain in 883, in which he professes to belong to the tribe of Dan (hence his name) and to hail from the east of Africa, near the Gulf of Aden. In the following fanciful travel account, Eldad relates how he arrived in the glorious kingdom of the Ten Lost Tribes, a land overflowing with precious gems, fertile livestock and exotic produce. Most imaginative is his description of how the various tribes, located on either side of the rumbling Sambatyon, communicated with one another.

A nd this was my going forth from the other side of the rivers of
Ethiopia. I and a Jew of the tribe of Asher entered a small ship to
trade with the shipmen and behold! at midnight, the Lord caused
a great and strong wind to arise and the ship was wrecked. Now
the Lord had prepared a box and I took hold of it and my
companion, seeing this, also took hold of that box, and we went
up and down with it, until the sea cast us among a people called
the Romranos, who are black Ethiopians, tall, without garment or
clothing upon them, cannibals, like unto the beasts of the field.

Now when we came to their country, they took hold of us, and
seeing that my companion was fat and healthy and pleasing,
slaughtered him and ate him... but me they took, for I was sick on
board ship, and they put me in chains until I should get fat and
well, and they brought me all kinds of good but forbidden food,
but I ate nothing and I hid the food, and when they asked me if I
had eaten I answered, yes, I had eaten.

And I was with them a long time until the Lord, blessed be He, performed a miracle on my behalf, for a great army from another place came upon those who had taken me captive; they spoiled and killed them and took me along with the captives. And those wicked men were fire-worshipers and I dwelt with them four years, and behold, every morning they made a great fire and bowed down and worshiped it. And they brought me to the province of Azania.

And a Jew, a merchant of the tribe of Issachar, found me and bought me for thirty-two gold pieces, and brought me back with him to his country. They live in the mountains of the seacoast and belong to the land of the Medes and the Persians. They fulfill the command, "The book of this Law shall not depart from your mouth." The yoke of sovereignty is not upon them, but only the yoke of the Law. Among them are leaders of hosts, but they fight with no man. They only dispute as to the law, and they live in peace and comfort and there is no disturber and no evil chance. They dwell in a country ten days' journey by ten days, and they have great flocks and camels and asses and slaves, but they do not rear horses.

They carry no weapons, except the slaughterer's knife, and there is not among them any oppression or robbery and, even if they should find on the road garments or money, they would not stretch forth their hand to take it....

And the sons of Zebulun are encamped in the hills of Paran and reach to the neighborhood of Issachar, and pitch tents made of hairy skins which come to them from the land of Armenia, and they reach up to the Euphrates, and they practice business and they observe the four death penalties inflicted by the court.

And the tribe of Reuben is over against them behind Mt. Paran, and there is peace and brotherhood between them, and they go together to war and make roads and divide the spoils amongst themselves, and they go on the highroads of the Kings of Media and Persia and they speak Hebrew and Persian, and they possess Scripture and Mishna, Talmud, and Aggadah, and every Sabbath they read the Law with accents, the text in Hebrew and the interpretation thereof in Persian.

And the tribe of Ephraim and the half-tribe of Manasseh are there in the mountains over against the city of Mecca, the stumbling block of the Ishmaelites. They are strong of body and of iron heart. They are horsemen and take the road and have no pity on their enemies, and their only livelihood comes of spoil. They are mighty men of war. One is match for a thousand.

And the tribe of Simeon and the half-tribe of Manasseh live in the country of the Babylonians, six months' journey away, and they are the most numerous of all of them, and they take tribute from five and twenty kingdoms and some Ishmaelites pay them tribute....

The tribes of Dan, Naphtali, Gad and Asher dwell in ancient Havilah, where gold is, and they trusted in their Maker, and the

Lord helped them. These tribes placed their hands on the neck of their enemies, and every year they make war with the seven kingdoms and seven countries. The names of these kingdoms are Tussina, Kamti, Duba, Tariogi, Takula, Karma and Kalom, and they are on the other side of the rivers of Ethiopia. These four tribes have gold and silver and precious stones, and much sheep and cattle and camels and asses, and they sow and they reap, and they dwell in tents, and, when they will, they journey and encamp in tents from border to border. And their king's name is Uzziel....

Every three months a different tribe goes out to war, and the tribe remains three months away, and all that they bring from the spoil of their enemies they divide among their own tribe. But the descendants of Samson, of the tribe of Dan are superior to all.

As to the tribe of Moses, our teacher, on whom be peace, the sea surrounds them, three months' journey by three months. They dwell in glorious houses and fine buildings and castles, and train elephants for themselves in their times of joy. No unclean thing is to be found with them, no unclean fowl, no unclean beast, no unclean cattle, no flies, no lice, no foxes, no scorpions, no serpents and no dogs. They have only sheep, oxen and fowls, and their sheep bring forth twice a year. They sow seed twice a year; they sow and they reap and they have gardens and olives and pomegranates and figs and all kinds of beans and cucumbers and melons and onions and garlic and barley and wheat, and from one comes forth a hundred.

They are of perfect faith and their Talmud is all in Hebrew. But they know not the Rabbis, for these were of the Second Temple and they did not reach them. And they can speak only the Holy Tongue and they all take ritual baths and never swear. And they are all Levites and have not among them either Priest or Israelite, and they abide in the sanctity of Moses, our teacher, the servant of God.

Moreover, they see no man and no men see them except these four tribes, who dwell on the other side of the river of Ethiopia. There is a place where these can see each other and speak if they cry out, but the River Sambatyon is between them, and they tell, "Thus it happened to us in war time," and they tell all Israel what happened to them. And when they want anything important, they have a kind of pigeon known among them, and they write their letters and fasten them to the wings or to the feet of the pigeon, and these cross the River Sambatyon and the pigeons come to their kings and their princes.

They also have very many precious stones and silver and gold, and they sow flax and they rear cochineal and make pleasant garments without end, and are fives times as numerous as those that came out of Egypt, for they are innumerable.

The breadth of that river is 200 cubits bowshot, and the river is full of large and small stones, and the sound of them rumbles like a great storm, like a tempest at sea and, in the night, the sound of it is heard a day's journey, and they have with them six wells and they all unite into one lake and therefrom they irrigate their land, and therein are clean, edible fish.

The river runs and the stones and sand rumble during the six working days, but on the seventh day it rests and is tranquil until the end of the Sabbath. And on the other side of the river, on the side where the four tribes dwell, is a fire which flames on the Sabbath and no man can approach within a mile....

These letters this Lord Eldad sent to Spain in the year 4043 (883), and this Lord Eldad was full of law and commandments.

May the Lord give him a good reward in this world and in the world to come.

Here ends the Book of Eldad the Danite. And these letters prince Eldad sent to Spain in the year 883.

3

Curiosity and the
Spanish Diplomat

Hisdai ibn Shaprut
to the King of the Khazars, c960

*Much has been written about the enigmatic Khazar kingdom which
existed in southern Russia from the 7th to 10th centuries. Some time
before the 9th century, the king and his court and part of the
population embraced Judaism, adhering to their adopted religion
until the kingdom was destroyed by the Russians.*

*According to tradition, this kingdom came to the attention of Hisdai
ibn Shaprut (915-990), a prominent Spanish Jew who served as
diplomat, physician and counselor to the caliph Abd al Rahman III.
His position made it possible for him to communicate with the King
of the Khazars, and to satisfy his curiosity as to whether this was an
independent kingdom established at long last by the Ten Tribes.*

*In the famous epistle ascribed to ibn Shaprut, he enquires as to the
nature of the kingdom and asks to which tribe of Israel the king
belongs. Scholars continue to debate the authenticity of this correspon-
dence.*

$\mathcal{I}$, Hisdai son of Isaac, may his memory be blessed, son of Ezra, belonging to the exiled Jews of Jerusalem in Spain, a servant of my Lord the King, bow to the earth before him and prostrate myself towards the abode of your Majesty from a distant land. I rejoice in your tranquillity and magnificence, and stretch forth my hands to God in Heaven that He may prolong your reign in Israel. But who am I? We, indeed, who are of the remnant of the captive Israelites, servants of my Lord the King, are dwelling peacefully in the land of our sojourning....

Let it be known, then, to the King my Lord, that the name of our land in which we dwell is called in the sacred tongue Sefarad, but in the language of the Arabs, the indwellers of the land, Alandalus [Andalusia], and the name of the capital of the kingdom, Cordoba. The length of it is 25,000 cubits, the breadth 10,000. It is situated at the left of the [Mediterranean] Sea which flows between your country and the Great [Atlantic] Sea and compasses the whole of your land....

I always ask the ambassadors [of the monarchs, who pass through our land] about our brethren, the Israelites, the remnant of the captivity, whether they have heard anything concerning the deliverance of those who have pined in bondage and had found no rest. At length, mercantile emissaries of Khorasan [a province of Persia adjoining Russia] told me that there is a kingdom of Jews who are called Khazars (and between Constantineh [Constantinople] and that country is a sea voyage of fifteen days, and many nations dwell between us and them). But I did not believe these words, for I thought that they told me such things to procure my good will and favor. I was therefore hesitating and doubtful until the ambassadors from Constantineh came with presents and a letter from their king to our king, whom I interrogated concerning this matter.

They answered me: "It is quite true; there is in that place a kingdom of Alcusari, distant from Constantineh a fifteen days' journey by sea, but many peoples are scattered through the land; the name of the king now reigning is Joseph; ships sometimes come from their country bringing fish, skins and wares of every kind; the men are our brethren and are honored by us; there is frequent communication between us by embassies and mutual gifts; they are very powerful; they maintain numerous armies, which they occasionally engage in expeditions." This account inspired me with hope, wherefore I bowed down and adored the God of Heaven....

Now, therefore, let it please your Majesty, I beseech you to have regard to the desires of your servant, and to command your scribes who are at hand to send back a reply from your distant land to your servant and to inform me fully concerning the condition of the Israelites and how they came to dwell there and to write to me about all the things namely: what is your state? what is the name of your land? what tribes inhabit it? what is the manner of the government? Would my lord the King also inform me as to the extent of his country, its length and breadth? What walled cities and what open towns it has; whether it be watered by artificial or natural means, and how far his dominion extends and also the number of his armies and their leaders?...

My lord sees that I enquire about this with no other object than that I may rejoice when I hear of the increase of the Holy People. I wish too that he would tell me of the number of the provinces over which he rules, the amount of tribute paid to him, if they give him tithes...if there are islands in the neighborhood and if any of their inhabitants conform to Judaism? If he judges over them? how he goes up to the house of God? with what peoples he wages war? whether he allows war to set aside the observance of the Sabbath? what kingdoms or nations are on his borders? what are their names and those of their territories?...

One thing more I ask of my lord, that he would tell me whether there is among you any computation concerning the final redemption which we have been awaiting for so many years, whilst we went from one captivity to another, from one exile to another.

How strong is the hope of him who awaits the realization of these events!

Blessed be the Lord of Israel who has not left us without a kinsman as defender nor suffered the Tribes of Israel to be without an independent kingdom. May my Lord the King prosper forever....

4

Learned Men and Savage Warriors

Benjamin of Tudela
Book of Travels, 12th century

The renowned 12th-century Spanish traveler Benjamin of Tudela set out in 1165, and traveled for several years to Jewish communities throughout the entire Mediterranean area and beyond. The record he kept of his travels is a primary source book for medieval historians, although most scholars agree that certain descriptions are of things heard rather than of things actually seen; in certain cases it is unlikely he even visited the country he describes.

Benjamin of Tudela claims to have come across various of the Ten Lost Tribes. He speculates that the men of Kheibar in El-Yemen are descendants of exiles from the tribes of Reuben, Gad and Manasseh, and those in Persia from the tribes of Dan, Asher, Zebulun, and Naphtali. His description of the Jews as fearless warriors who go forth to make war and to pillage and who suffer not the yoke of the Gentiles, was a comforting fantasy in a reality much less idyllic.

$\mathcal{F}$rom Hillah it is a journey of twenty-one days by way of the deserts to the land of Saba, which is called the land El-Yemen, lying at the side of the land of Shinar which is towards the North.

Here dwell the Jews called Kheibar, the men of Teima. And Teima is their seat of government where Rabbi Hanan the Nasi rules over them. It is a great city, and the extent of their land is sixteen days' journey. It is surrounded by mountains - the mountains of the north. The Jews own many large fortified cities. The yoke of the Gentiles is not upon them. They go forth to pillage and to capture booty from distant lands in conjunction with the Arabs, their neighbors and allies. These Arabs dwell in tents and they make the desert their home.

All the neighbors of these Jews go in fear of them. Among them are husbandmen and owners of cattle; their land is extensive, and they have in their midst learned and wise men. They give tithe of all they possess unto the scholars who sit in the house of learning, also to poor Israelites and to recluses, who are the mourners of Zion and Jerusalem, and who do not eat meat nor taste wine, and sit clad in garments of black. They dwell in caves or underground houses and fast each day with the exception of the Sabbaths and Festivals, and implore mercy of the Holy One, blessed be He, on account of the exile of Israel, praying that He may take pity upon them, and upon all the Jews, the men of Teima, for the sake of His great name....

There are here about forty large towns and 200 hamlets and villages. The principal city is Tanai, and in all the districts together there are about 300,000 Jews. The city of Tanai is well fortified, and in the midst thereof the people sow and reap.... And Tilmas is likewise a great city; it contains about 100,000 Jews. It is well-fortified, and is situated between two high mountains. There are wise, discreet and rich men among the inhabitants.

From Tilmas to Kheibar it a three days' journey. People say that the men of Kheibar belong to the tribes of Reuben, Gad and Manasseh, whom Shalmaneser, king of Assyria, led hither into captivity. They have built strongly-fortified cities, and make war upon all other kingdoms. No man can readily reach their territory, because it is a march of eighteen days' journey through the desert, which is altogether uninhabited, so that no one can enter the land. Kheibar is a very large city with 50,000 Jews. In it are learned men and great warriors who wage war with the men of Shinar and of the land of the north, as well as with the bordering countries....

Thence [in the confines of Persia] it takes twenty-eight days to the mountains of Naisabur, by the river Gozan. And there are men of Israel in the land of Persia who say that in the mountains of Naisabur four of the tribes of Israel dwell, namely, the tribe of Dan, the tribe of Zebulun, the tribe of Asher, and the tribe of Naphtali, who were included in the first captivity of Shalmaneser, King of Assyria, as it is written (II Kings 17:6): "And he put them in Halah and in Habor by the river of Gozan and in the cities of the Medes."

The extent of their land is twenty days' journey, and they have cities and large villages in the mountains; the river Gozan forms the boundary on the one side. They are not under the rule of the Gentiles, but they have a prince of their own, whose name is Joseph Amarkala the Levite. There are scholars among them. And they sow and reap and go forth to war as far as the land of Cush by way of the desert.

They are in league with the Kofar-al-Turak, who worship the wind and live in the wilderness, and who do not eat bread, nor drink wine, but live on raw uncooked meat. They have no noses, and in lieu thereof they have two small holes through which they breathe. They eat animals both clean and unclean, and they are very friendly towards the Israelites.

Fifteen years ago they overran the country of Persia with a large army and took the city of Rayy; they smote it with the edge of the sword, took all the spoil thereof, and returned by way of the wilderness. Such an invasion had not been known in the land of Persia for many years....

In Search
of Paradise

Obadiah Jare da Bertinoro

to his family, 1488-1489

Obadiah Jare of Bertinoro was one of the most distinguished Italian rabbis of his time. His commentary on the Mishnah (collection of oral laws) remains a standard work to this day. The letters he wrote to his family, describing the communities he visited during his voyage to the Holy Land (1487-1490), have been preserved and translated into several languages. Obadiah appears to have resided in Jerusalem until his death around 1500, and a subsequent traveler reports he was a leader in the Jewish community in Palestine.

The following brief selections from his letters relate to news he received concerning the Sambatyon. They also make mention of the popular Prester John story which circulated in Europe and Asia for several centuries. According to this legend, somewhere beyond the Moslem countries there lived a powerful Christian priest and monarch named Prester John, who ruled over a vast and wealthy empire, home to the Ten Lost Tribes (see Introduction, pg. 8).

To his father, Jerusalem, Aug. 1488

I made enquiries concerning the Sambatyon, and I hear from
one who has been informed, that a man has come from the
kingdom of Prester John and has related that there are high
mountains and valleys there which can be traversed in a ten days'
journey, and which are certainly inhabited by descendants of
Israel. They have five princes or kings, and have carried on great
wars against the Johannites (Ethiopians) for more than a century,
but, unfortunately, the Johannites prevailed and Ephraim was
beaten. The Johannites penetrated into their country and the
remembrance of Israel had almost died away in those places, for
an edict was issued against those who remained, prohibiting the
exercise of their religious duties as severe as that which Antiochus
issued in the time of the Hasmoneans. But God had mercy.

Other kings succeeded in India who were not so cruel as their predecessors; and it is said that the former glory of the Jews is now in a measure restored; they have again become numerous, and though they still pay tribute to the Johannites they are not entirely subject to them. Four years ago, it is said, they again made war with their neighbors, when they plundered their enemies and made many prisoners. The enemy, on the other hand, took some of them prisoners, and sold them as slaves; a few of these were brought to Cairo and redeemed by the Jews there. I saw two of them in Cairo; they were black but not so black as the negroes. It was impossible to learn from them whether they belonged to the Karaites or the Rabbanites....

Finished in haste in Jerusalem, the Holy City. May it soon be rebuilt in our days. From your son, Obadiah Jare
On the 8th of Elul, 5248 (1488)

To his brother, Jerusalem, Sept. 1489

Jews have come here [to the Holy Land] from Aden; Aden is said to be the site of the garden of Eden: it lies southeast of Ethiopia, but the Red Sea separates them. These Jews say that in their country there are many large Jewish communities, that the king is an Arab, and is very kindly disposed to the Jews, and that the country is very large and beautiful, bearing many splendid fruits, of kinds which are not to be found among us. Where Paradise was actually situated they do not know. They sow in the month of Adar (March) and reap in Kislev (December). The rainy season there is from Passover to the month of Av (August). It is in consequence of the great quantity of rain that falls there that the Nile rises in the month of Av.

Its inhabitants are somewhat black. The Jews do not possess the books of the Talmud. They are all, from great to small, well-versed in the works of Maimonides, for they occupy themselves principally with studying them.

The Jews told us also that it is now well-known through Arabian merchants that the river Sambatyon is eighty days' journey from them in the wilderness, and, surrounds the whole land like a thread, and that the descendants of Jacob dwell there. This river throws up stones and sand, and rests only on the Sabbath, therefore no Jew, who is traveling in that country, can cross over it, for otherwise he would violate the Sabbath. It is a tradition among them that the descendants of Moses dwell there, all pure and innocent as angels, and no evil-doer is in their midst.

On the other side of the Sambatyon the Children of Israel are as numerous as the sand of the sea, and there are many kings and princes among them, but they are not so pure and holy as those surrounded by the stream. The Jews of Aden relate all this with a certain confidence, as if it were well known, and no one ever doubted the truth of their assertions.

An old Ashkenazi Rabbi who was born and educated here [in Jerusalem] tells me that he remembers how even in his youth, Jews came from Aden, and narrated everything literally as these do. The Jews of Aden also say that the Israelites dwelling on the borders of their territory, of whom I wrote in my first letter, are now at war with the people of Prester John [the Ethiopians], and that some of them have been taken prisoners and brought to Cairo. I have seen some of these with my own eyes; these Jews are a month's journey in the wilderness from the others who live on the Sambatyon.

The Christians who come from the territory of the Johannites relate that the Jews there, who are at war with the people of Prester John, have suffered great defeats, and we are very anxious to know if these accounts are really true, which God forfend. May the Lord always protect his people and his servants!...

Sent in haste from Jerusalem,
Elul the 27th, 5249 (1489)

From your brother, Obadiah Jare

- 6 -

A Visit
to the Pope

David Reubeni
Diary account, 1520s

One of the most romantic figures of the 16th century was the Jewish adventurer David Reubeni. The diary account of his travels through Europe and North Africa (1522-1525), replete with exaggerated stories about luxurious expenditures, great treasures and wicked servants, has been the subject of several novels.

In 1523, after spending time in Alexandria, Jerusalem and Damascus, Reubeni sailed for Venice. His visit to Venice, his first historically recorded appearance, aroused intense messianic hopes among his brethren. Reubeni claimed to be the son of a King Solomon and the brother of a King Joseph who ruled the lost tribes of Reuben and Gad and half the tribe of Manasseh in the desert of Habor (mentioned in the book of II Kings as the place to which the kingdom of Israel was exiled). He, Reubeni, the commander-in-chief of these tribesmen, asked the Jews of Venice to aid in an important mission to the Pope, and several notables complied with his request.

In 1524 Reubeni arrived in Rome, riding on a white horse. Reubeni proposed an alliance between Pope Clement VII and the Christian nations against the Turks: If the European nations would supply the ammunition, his brother would raise the military manpower from his army of Israelites. Thus the Israelites could recover Palestine from the Turkish Moslems (who had conquered Jerusalem in 1517), and the Christian world could thwart their advance towards the West.

According to the following selection from Reubeni's diary, the Pope, duly impressed, became Reubeni's patron, giving him a letter of recommendation to King John III of Portugal and to the mythical Ethiopian king Prester John (see Introduction, pg. 8). Several Jewish bankers in Rome supplied Reubeni with funds to support his messianic mission.

In Portugal, the king gave Reubeni a splendid welcome, as did the Marranos (New Christians, living secretly as Jews) who were convinced he heralded the coming Messiah. He likewise cultivated contacts with the sultan of Fez and the Jews of North Africa. The unrest he caused began to arouse suspicions in Portugal that he was seeking to incite the Marranos, and he was expelled. Reubeni's diary tells of his further adventures in France and Italy, where he succeeded in arousing messianic fervor as well. He was eventually arrested on charges of seducing the New Christians to embrace Judaism; he perished in prison in Spain.

Several scholars question the authorship of Reubeni's diary; others consider many parts to be fictitious, based on myths prevalent at the time. Nonetheless, his writings reflect a deeply religious nature, ingenious political acumen, and an unswerving obsession with raising the spirit of the downtrodden Jews with promises of redemption.

Ho Preſte Joam das indias.

Verdadera informaçam das terras do Preſte
Joam ſegundo vio τ eſcreueo ho padre Franciſco Aluarez capellá del Rey noſſo
ſenhor. Agora nouaméte impreſſo por mandado do dito ſenhor em caſa de Luis
Rodriguez liureiro de ſua alteza.

In Rome:

I, David, the son of King Solomon, of righteous memory, from the wilderness of Habor, entered the gate of the City of Rome on the 15th day of Adar, 1524... I went to the Pope's palace, riding on horseback, and my servant before me, and the Jews also came with me... I and the Cardinal went to the apartment of the Pope, and I spoke with him, and he received me graciously and said, "The matter is from the Lord"; and I said to him, "King Joseph and his elders ordered me to tell you to make peace between the Emperor and the French King, by all means, for it will be well with you and them if you do so; and write for me a letter to these two kings, and they will help us and we will help them; and write also for me to King Prester John [i.e. the King of Ethiopia].

The Pope answered me, "I cannot make peace between these two kings, but if you need help, the King of Portugal will assist you, and I will write to him and he will do all. His land is near your country and they are accustomed to travel on the great sea every year, more than those in the lands of those other kings."

...Then I and Rabbi Daniel of Pisa left the Pope, happy and of good courage, and we went in peace to my home.... Within a few days, the Pope sent for Rabbi Daniel of Pisa and me, and we went before him and I stayed with him for about two hours. He spoke to me saying, "I have given you a letter to King Prester John, and I have also written to the King of Portugal, and I have written to the Christians whose country you will pass so that they should help you, and honor you for God's sake and my sake." He further said, "Be strong and of good courage and fear not, for God is with you." And I said to him, "There is none before me but the Almighty and you, and I am prepared to serve you all the days of my life, and also King Joseph my brother and all my people's sons are inclined to you." And the Pope ordered that they should give me a sign and shield to show to King Joseph my brother, and he also gave me one hundred golden ducats. I would not take the money, but only under compulsion when he said, "Take it for your servants." I left the Pope and returned home in peace and joy and a good heart.

In Portugal:

A great Moslem lord, a Judge of the King of Fez, came to me. He had been sent by this King to the King of Portugal, and is an honorable man, a friend of the Jews. He has ten servants.... He asked me about my country and I answered that it is in the wilderness of Habor and that there are thirty myriad Jews living there, and King Joseph, my brother, rules over them and he has seventy counselors and many lords, and I am military lord over ways and war. And the Judge said to me, "What do you seek from this kingdom that you have come from the east to the west?" I answered that from our youth we are trained in war, and our war is with the sword and lance and bow, and that we wished to go, with God's help, to Jerusalem to capture the land of Israel from the Moslems, for the end and salvation has arrived, and that I have come to seek wise craftsmen who know how to make weapons and firearms that they should come to my land and make them and teach our soldiers.

The Judge was much amazed at this...and said to me, "Do you wish to write a letter for me to give to the King of Fez?" I answered, "I need not write, but you can say all this to him by word of mouth, and give him from me a thousand greetings and say to him that the Jews under his rule should be protected by him, and that he should honor them and this will be the beginning of peace between us and him, between our seed and his seed." The Judge also asked me, "What will you do with the Jews in all the lands of the west?" I replied that we shall first take the Holy Land and its surroundings, and that then our captains of host will go forth to the west and east to gather the dispersed of Israel; whoever is wise among the Moslem kings will take the Jews under his rule and bring them to Jerusalem, and he will have much honor, greater than that of all the Moslem kings, and God will deliver up all the kingdoms to the king of Jerusalem....

After that, I called the man that spoke Arabic, the interpreter between me and the King, and said to him, "I am from the wilderness of Habor and we have thirty times ten thousand Jews there (May the Lord increase them a thousand fold!). They are the sons of Reuben and Gad and of half the tribe of Manasseh, and King Joseph, my brother, is their king, and I am the lord of his host. The other nine and a half tribes are in the land of the blacks in Ethiopia, in four places. The sons of Moses are in another place and live on the River Sambatyon, beside the two tribes of Simeon and Benjamin, who reside at the head of the River Nile and the white river behind it. They are between two rivers, beyond the Kingdom of Sheba. These two tribes send men to us, and we send men to them, and they tell us what they hear and know of the other tribes in the land of the blacks which are near to them, and our country is far from them, as we are in the east."

Where the Waters
Run Sacred

Gershon ben Eliezer Halevi
Yiddls of Prague
Sacred Epistles, 1624

Gershon ben Eliezer Yiddls from Prague traveled to the Holy Land in 1624, visiting several lands in Africa and Asia on his way; his experiences are recorded in a book he called Sacred Epistles. Scholars have identified sections as having been copied from other travelogues and embellished with considerable exaggeration.

In one of his most imaginative tales, Yiddls relates how he joined a caravan carrying iron from Salonika and, near the border of Greater India, came across the mythical River Sambatyon, flowing ever more wondrous and miraculous.

Yiddls' epistle also makes mention of the popular Prester John story which circulated in Europe and Asia for several centuries (see Introduction, pg. 8).

T here are those who told me there is a place where the Ten Tribes
dwell and they have kings and princes and leaders, and lack
nothing that is good other than the Holy Temple and Prophecy,
and that they live a peaceful and content life and many nations pay
them a yearly tax. And if any nation rebels against them, they go
to war and subdue them. There are those who say the place of
their dwelling is near the River Sambatyon, and there are those
who say beyond the River Gozan; and there are those who say
beyond the hills of darkness....

The truth is that I myself did not fully believe this, given the fact
of our bitter exile. And so, I swear to you by the living God who
created all living things, because I would not lie one letter of what
I am about to write here....

When I traveled by sea from Alexandria to Salonika, it was told to me that a caravan from a distant land had come to buy iron, and I asked from where these people came? I was told from the land of Hovesh, and they carry the iron from Salonika to a land beyond the River Sambatyon... and I decided that since I understood the language and ways of these people, I would travel along with them, whatever befalls me, and I asked if I too might join [the chief merchant] to buy iron so as to earn a bit of money.

And if I wished to tell you at length of my trip through countries, cities, seas and deserts, a thousand pages would not suffice, and so I will tell you in short....

As we approached the city near the Sambatyon we heard sounds of confusion and a great noise like thunder, and the closer we got to the city the louder the sound. And I asked what this terrible sound was I was hearing, and I was told that it came from the River Sambatyon. And as we approached the city, the people said we could not leave the walls of the city as the King Prester John had placed guards along the shores of the river, because of the terrible oppression with which the Jews oppressed the Johannites. And the King Prester John is an Ishmaelite, and we were forced to unload our goods and we were delayed there three weeks....

And when it was two hours before the Sabbath, I no longer heard the noise or the tumult, and I was told that this was the nature of the River, which storms all the days of creation, and close to the Sabbath quiets down and rests until the Sabbath has ended...and not even the smallest pebble can be seen, only sand, white as snow and very thin.

When the Sabbath ends, it begins to storm and make noise as
before, and to cast about large stones up to the height of a house.
I heard that the nations who live near the river do not drink from
its waters, nor do they let any animal drink from it as it said the
water is sacred. Anyone with boils or rashes on his head goes there
to rinse in its waters and is cured, and this proves to them as well
that its waters are sacred.

The width of the river is 17 parasangs. And the land itself is great
in width and breadth, and there is every sort of fruit, meat, fish,
and plentiful poultry, and the people never wear black garments.
And there are fruit trees and every sort of spice. And I was also
told that one must cross two more lands from Prester John's
kingdom to reach the River Sambatyon, and in these lands a
person who kills an animal is sentenced to death like a murderer.

It is said that beyond the river live the Jews and they have four-
and-twenty kings, and each king has his own land and among
them are large and fortified cities and countless villages. And one
king rules over them all, and he is a terribly brave warrior, and
when he rides on his donkey, one hundred and fifty thousand
armed warriors follow behind, with armor and spears. And their
horses are large and terrible and always look forward and back,
and they are trained in war, they bite and trample and kill anyone
who comes near. They feed on sheep and cattle – cooked in thin
pieces, and drink wine, and when they eat and drink no man can

approach....

Two hours before the Sabbath they pass before the River
Sambatyon and, though you may find this hard to believe, the
speed of the horses is so great, that they complete the crossing of
this wide river before the Sabbath has begun; and they snort
incessantly and celebrate the Sabbath on this side of the river,
which is the land of Prester John.

And here there are many lands and cities and communities which
touch the border of Greater India. And beyond the river, the Jews
make sure that their enemies do not approach them, and anyone
who crosses and comes upon them they immediately kill, except
the Ishmaelite traders. Their horses, which we mentioned, can
stand for three days in one place, and their riders load them up
with all sorts of war weapons and sacks of grain and fine spices,
that they need not get down at all from their horses....

It is said that all the men and women know a trade so as to
support themselves with ease, and the land lacks nothing in crops,
fruit, delicacies and other commodities, anything you might
mention, as well as silver, gold, and an abundance of precious
stones – everything except for iron of which they have none at all.
Ishmaelite merchants bring them iron, and from this they make
their weapons....

- 8 -

The Native Americans and the Second Coming

Menasseh ben Israel

to John Dury, Chaplain to Mary, Princess of Orange, 1649

John Dury, chaplain to Mary, Princess of Orange, and Oliver
Cromwell's unofficial agent in the Netherlands, addressed a letter to
the Dutch Jewish scholar Menasseh ben Israel in 1649. Dury posed
several questions regarding reports of Jewish tribes living in South
America (Montezinos' report, 1644). Like other theologians during
the turbulent period of the Puritan Revolution, Dury believed that
the restoration of all Jews to the Holy Land was a requirement for
the Second Coming of Christ; if redemption were to take place, the
Lost Tribes had to be found in order to participate in the collective
return.

Menasseh ben Israel's response, which supports the discovery of the
Lost Ten Tribes in South America, formed the basis of his work,
The Hope of Israel. He dedicated the Latin edition of this work to
the English parliament in a political effort to solicit their goodwill
and to permit the return of the Jews to England (they had been
expelled in 1290). Menasseh ben Israel played on the messianic
sentiments of the English parliamentarians, suggesting that by
allowing the Jews to return, they would in essence be completing the
prerequisite for the Second Coming, i.e., the dispersion of the Jews to
"the end of the earth" (Deut. 28:64; "Angle Terre" which is the
meaning of "England").

Amsterdam, 25 November 1649

*B*y the occasion of the questions you propose unto me concerning this adjourned Narrative of Mr. Antonio Montezinos, I, to give you satisfaction, have written a treatise instead of a letter, which I shortly will publish and whereof you shall receive as many copies as you desire. In this treatise I handle of the first inhabitants of America which I believe were of the Ten Tribes; moreover that they were scattered also in other countries, that they keep their true religion, as hoping to return into the Holy Land in due time....

Amsterdam, 23 December 1649

I declare how that our Israelites were the first finders out of America; not regarding the opinions of other men, which I thought good to refute in a few words only; and I think that the Ten Tribes live not only there, but also in other lands scattered every where; these never did come back to the Second Temple, and keep till this day still the Jewish Religion, seeing all the prophecies which speak of their bringing back unto their native soil must be fulfilled:

So then at their appointed time, all the Tribes shall meet from all the parts of the world into two Provinces, namely Assyria and Egypt, nor shall their kingdom be any more divided, but they shall have one Prince – the Messiah, the Son of David. I do also set forth the Inquisition of Spain, and rehearse diverse of our Nation, and also of Christians, Martyrs, who in our times suffered several sorts of torments, and then having showed with what great honours our Jews have been graced also by several Princes who profess Christianity.

I prove at large, that the day of the promised Messiah unto us doth draw near, upon which occasion I explain many Prophecies....

- 9 -

Behold,
The Messiah!

Nathan of Gaza

to his brethren in Israel, 1665

When Shabbetai Zevi, the self-proclaimed Messiah from Turkey, arrived in the Holy Land in 1665, he journeyed to Gaza to meet a charismatic young scholar named Nathan. Nathan, who was reputed to be able to read souls and dispel demons, and who claimed to have experienced a vision of Shabbetai Zevi as the Messiah, became his most ardent follower and prophet.

A master in public relations, Nathan sent letters to Italy, Holland, Germany and Poland announcing the Messiah. Several factors contributed to his most prominent role in spreading belief in Shabbetai Zevi, among them: his outstanding literary ability; his brilliant use of symbols; and the fact that his messianic call came from the Holy Land, the center that represented pure spirituality at its most intense.

In the following ingenious letter, Nathan outlines the course of events which will take place from the present moment until complete redemption is achieved; Shabbetai Zevi is to travel to the Sambatyon, where he will marry Rebecca (the 13-year-old daughter of the resuscitated Moses) and bring back the Lost Tribes. Copies of this circular letter, composed in 1665, found their way at the speed of light, throughout the Jewish world. Within a few weeks they were read aloud, amidst great rejoicing, in Salonika, Constantinople, Venice, Leghorn, Amsterdam, Paris, London, Posen and Lemberg.

*H*ear ye, Brethren in Israel, that our Messiah is come to life in
the city of Ismir and his name is Shabbetai Zevi. Soon he will
show forth his kingdom to all and will take the royal crown from
the head of the Sultan and place it on his own. Like a Canaanitish
slave shall the King of the Turks walk behind him, for to Shabbetai is the power and the glory.

But when nine months have passed, our Messiah shall vanish
from before the eyes of Israel, and no one shall be able to say
whether he is alive or dead. But he will cross the river Sambatyon
which, as all men know, no mortal has ever crossed.

There he will marry the daughter of Moses and our Messiah shall
ride forth to Jerusalem with Moses and all the Jews of old
mounted on horses. He himself shall ride on a dragon whose

bridle rein shall be a snake with seven heads.

On his way he will be attacked by Gog and Magog, the enemies of Israel, with a mighty army. But the Messiah shall not conquer his enemies with ordinary weapons made by men. Nay, with the breath of his nostril shall he rout them, and by his word alone shall he utterly destroy them.

And when he is entered into Jerusalem, God will send down a temple of gold and precious stones from heaven, and it shall fill the city with its brilliance, and in it shall the Messiah offer up sacrifice as High Priest. And in that day shall the dead throughout the world rise from their graves. I hasten to tell you these tidings.